THE SCENIC MANX COOKBOOK

PAMELA M. CROWE

FANNAG PRESS

Published by
Fannag Press
P.O. Box 100
Port Erin
Isle of Man.

First Edition 1989
© Fannag Prress

Printed by Ramsey Print Ltd.

ISBN No 1-871718-00-7

'Gem of God's Earth'; how well the Manx National Anthem describes our Island, 220 square miles, a stepping stone set in the Irish Sea between England and Ireland.

Ringed with beautiful beaches and rocky coves, the Island rises to wild mountain moorland through a series of lovely glens. Abundent sporting facilities, historic castles and ancient sites complete this charming setting.

By law, the Island does not allow the use of additives in much of our home produced food, award winning cheese, flours milled in the historic Laxey Mill, ice cream, the famous Manx kipper, fresh fish from the sea, plentiful fruit and vegetables and ale brewed by traditional methods - truly a dream island for the discerning drinker! We even have Manx whiskey, clear as our sparkling mountain streams.

The author, married to a Manxman for 25 years, has collected, devised or acquired these recipes over the years.

CONTENTS

Soups.. *1 - 3*

Fish & Shellfish... *4 - 16*

Cheese Dishes .... *17 - 20*

Meat, Game & Poultry..................................... *21 - 32*

Breads... *33 - 34*

Cakes.. *35 - 39*

Puddings.. *40 - 43*

Wines, Jams & Sweets .... *44 - 48*

Index.. *50 - 51*

MANX BROTH

8oz/250g Shin Beef
1 Marrow Bone (ask the butcher to saw this in half)
Salt
2oz/50g Pearl Barley
Vegetables (in season), diced (carrots, onions, cabbage, leeks, turnip)
Sprig of Thyme
2 tbsp fresh Parsley, chopped (do not use dried parsley, if you've no parsley growing in the garden, leave it out)

Cut the shin into small pieces, place in a pan with marrow bone, barley and salt. Leave to soak overnight, do not pour off this liquid. Next day gradually bring the bone, beef and barley to the boil, reduce to simmer, and simmer for 1 hour. Add the vegetables and herbs, continue to simmer until the vegetables are cooked. Remove the marrow bone and leave to cool.

Skim the fat off the broth before serving or freezing.

Serve with a chunk of warm brown wheaten bread and a pat of Manx butter.

P.O.W. SOUP

During World War 2, the Port Erin/Port St. Mary area was used as an internment camp for nearly 4,000 women; outnumbering the locals 2 to 1. Nearly 10,000 men were interned on the Island in camps in Douglas, Peel and Ramsey.

1 Ham Shank (soaked overnight)
14oz/400g tin chopped Tomatoes
4oz/125g Spaghetti, broken into 2"/5cm pieces
2 medium Onions
Any other Vegetables (courgettes, carrots, celery, leeks, cabbage, turnip)
1 clove of garlic (if liked)
2 tsp Mixed Herbs
1oz/25g Manx Butter
Black Pepper to taste

Remove all skin and excess fat from the ham shank, cover with fresh water and bring to the boil, simmer until the ham is cooked (I use a pressure cooker to save time). When the ham is falling from the bone, remove the shank from the stock and chop the meat into bite size pieces. Remove all the bones. In another pan or skillet, melt half the butter and gently sweat the onions, garlic and other vegetables, tipping them into the stock as you go. Add the chopped tomatoes, spaghetti and herbs to the stock and simmer gently until all the vegetables are well cooked. Tip in the cooked ham.

Serve with a topping of finely grated Manx Cheshire Cheese.

CHEESE AND ONION SOUP

6oz/165g Manx Mild Cheddar Cheese, grated
2 medium sized Onions
1 pint/600ml Chicken Stock
½ pint/285ml Milk
2oz/50g Butter
2oz/50g Flour
Salt and Pepper to taste

Finely chop the onions, simmer gently in the chicken stock. Melt the butter in another large pan, add the flour, mix until smooth, gradually stir in the milk and while stirring, add the cheese. When the onions are completely cooked, gradually add them and the stock to the cheese sauce. A balloon whisk is useful at this stage, as it is essential to blend in the stock and onions smoothly. Add salt and pepper to taste. Serve this delicious creamy soup hot, sprinkled with a little chopped chives.

Do not allow this soup to boil.

PRIDDHAS N' HERRIN'
or
SPUDS N' HERRIN'

Salt Herrings
Potatoes
1 glass of Buttermilk

Scrub the spuds, place in a large pan, cover with water, do not add salt, bring to boil. Wash n' rinse the herring, pour away most of the spud water, place herrin' on the spuds and cover with a tight fitting lid. Heat gently whilst the herrin' cooks in the steam of the spuds. When cooked, serve on a large platter; alongside a bowl of sliced raw onion.

A glass of cool buttermilk is the traditional accompaniment for this meal.
Every Manx home had a herrin' crock to salt down the fish for this traditional meal.
Salt herring is now available from the fishmonger for this really simple tasty meal.

ANNIE'S SOUSED HERRIN'

8 fresh Manx Herrings
1 thinly sliced Onion
½ pint/275ml Vinegar with a pinch of Peppercorns
½ pint/275ml Water

Cut the heads and tails off the herrin', ease out the backbone with your thumb. Remove as many bones as possible. Wash the herrin' well and pat dry. Place a couple of onion rings in each herrin' and roll. Place these in an overproof dish with fin upwards. Pour in the vinegar, water and peppercorns. Cook in the centre of the oven for 1-1½ hours on Gas Mark 2/150° C/300° F. Alternatively microwave for approximately 6 minutes and brown under the grill until golden brown.

Serve cold with a fresh Manx tomato salad.

I can never wait that long, so I throw a couple of spuds in the oven whilst the herrin' are cooking. A hot soused herrin' with a baked spud is one of my favourite meals.

THE FAMOUS MANX KIPPER

Herring fishing was a vital component of the Manx economy from the Middle Ages. In the thirteenth century, both the Lord of Man and the Church had title to shares in the catch. Exports began in the sixteenth century, and at one period vast quantities of salted and smoked herring were sent to feed the plantation slaves of America and the West Indies.

By the early nineteenth century, the Manx kipper was making its mark, and it has been to the forefront ever since.

No kipper can, by law, be described as Manx if dye is used. The traditional methods are, therefore, still used. The herrings are split and placed in brine for a short time, and then hung on frames of tenterhooks and put in the kiln for smoking. The kilns hold up to 30,000 pairs. The secret of achieving the best kippers in the world is the period of smoking, the handling in the kiln and the hardwood chippings used for the smoking. The quality of the Peel Herring was ideal for this process, thus Peel became the home of the world famous Manx Kipper.

KIPPER KEDGEREE

1lb/450g boned Manx Kipper fillets, skinned
2oz/50g Butter
8oz/225g cooked Long Grain Rice
2fl oz/50ml Double Cream
4 hardboiled Eggs, finely chopped
¼ tsp Salt
½ tsp freshly ground Black Pepper
1 tsp Mustard

With a sharp knife cut the kipper fillets into small pieces. In a large, deep frying pan melt the butter over a moderate heat. When the foam subsides, add the kipper pieces and fry them for 3-4 minutes, turning them frequently or until they are lightly browned. Add the rice and stir in the cream and chopped eggs. Add the salt, pepper and mustard and cook, stirring constantly for 3 minutes or until the mixture is heated through. Remove the pan from the heat and turn the kedgeree into a large warmed serving dish.

Serve at once with lemon wedges.

Delicious for a fork supper, this was originally a breakfast dish.

MANX KIPPER PATE

1½ lb/650g Manx Kippers
8oz/225g Butter or Margarine
Pepper
Lemon juice

Put the kippers in a jug deep enough to take them with a little room to spare. Pour in boiling water to cover them. Cover the top with a saucer and stand the jug in a warm place for 5-10 minutes. Drain the kippers and allow to become cold. Remove the bones and the skin. Warm the butter to soften but not to melt. Add it to the kippers and put in an electric blender until smooth. Alternatively, rub the kippers through a sieve and work in the butter. Add the pepper and lemon juice to taste. Pour into individual pots and top with melted butter.

    Decorate with parsley. Serve with lemon wedges and hot, brown toast.

    As an alternative lunch dish I add 5oz of cottage cheese into the sieved mixture and serve turned out onto a mixed salad.

KIPPER SALAD

1 medium Apple
1 tsp Lemon Juice
2 sticks Celery, chopped
3oz /75g Beetroot, cubed
6oz/165g fresh Manx Kippers, cooked, cold and boned
4fl oz/120 ml Orange Juice
2 medium Tomatoes, sliced
2 inch wedge Cucumber, sliced
1 tblsp chopped Spring Onions

Quarter the apple, remove and discard the core, slice the fruit and toss in the lemon juice. Mix together the apple, celery, beetroot and kipper pieces. Pour over the orange juice and toss well. Arrange the slices of tomato and cucumber alternately round the edges of the serving plate, pile the kipper salad in the centre and sprinkle with the chopped spring onions.

    A slimming meal, but full of nutrition.

KIPPER MOUSSE

12oz/340g Manx Kipper fillets
½ pint/275ml Single Cream
1oz/25g Butter
1oz/25g Plain Flour
½ pint/275ml Milk
Salt and Pepper
2 Eggs, separated
½ oz/15g Gelatine
Juice of Half Lemon
2 tblsp Water

Poach the kipper fillets until cooked through. Cool and remove any bones. Break up the fish and put into a liquidiser with the cream. Blend until smooth. Melt the butter and stir in the flour, and cook over a low heat, add the milk, and bring to the boil, stirring well. Remove from the heat, season with salt and pepper and beat in the egg yolks. Sprinkle the gelatine on the lemon juice and water in a cup. Stand in a pan of hot water and stir until the gelatine becomes syrupy. Stir this into the white sauce. Cool to lukewarm and fold the sauce into the kipper mixture. Whisk the egg whites to soft peaks and fold into the fish. Spoon into a 1½ pint/750ml souffle dish or into individual dishes. Leave in a cool place to set and chill before serving.

The mousse may be garnished with slices of cucumber or lemon.

Half the price of salmon mousse, and twice as tasty.

PEEL HOT POT

1oz/25g Brown or Rye Bread Crumbs
1lb/450g Potatoes, peeled
2 Onions, peeled
3 Manx Kippers, skinned and filleted
Freshly ground Black Pepper
2 Eggs
½ pint/300ml Milk, or enough to barely cover
1oz/25g Butter

To Garnish and serve
Lemon Wedges and Parsley Sprigs

Crumble the bread into fine crumbs, set aside. Slice the onions and the potatoes, set aside. Butter a 750ml/1½ pint ovenproof dish and dust with the crumbs. Make layers of the potatoes, onions and kippers, seasoning the layers with the pepper. Finish with a layer of potatoes, arranged in a circle. Beat the eggs and milk with a little pepper and pour over the potatoes. Dot the butter over the top. Bake in a moderate oven Gas Mark 4/180° C/350° F for 30 minutes. Reduce heat to Gas Mark 3/160° C/325° F for a further 30 minutes or until the potatoes are tender.

Serve hot, garnished with lemon and parsley.

COOKING MANX FISH

Manx fish is of superb quality and is best cooked by simply grilling. However, fish can be so easily spoilt by under or overcooking. Test for readiness by pressing gently in the thickest part, the flesh will readily separate from the bone when cooked. When cooking fillets or cutlets the presence of a white 'curd' is an indication that the fish is cooked.

To Grill Manx Fish

Clean and dry the fish, brush liberally with melted butter and season with salt and pepper, score deep gashes across the fish to allow the heat to penetrate. Cook the fish quite slowly turning carefully until done. Six to 8 minutes for thin fillets and between 10 and 15 minutes for larger fish.

A superb meal a fresh Manx trout, turbot, brill or plaice, simply grilled, simply delicious.

QUEENIES PUIRT LE MOIRREY

16 fresh Queenies
1½ -2oz/3-4 tblsp Butter
1½ -2oz/3-4 tblsp Flour
½ pint/300 ml Milk
Salt and Pepper
1 Onion, thinly sliced
Wine Glass of White Wine
A little Paprika
Chopped Parsley
Scallop Shells
2lb/950g creamed Potatoes

Edge the scallop shells with piped potato and place under low grill to keep warm and brown.

Clean the queenies and remove the beards but not the tongues. Cut queenies into mouth sized bites and set aside. Soften the onion in the butter and make a roux with it and the flour. Thin with the milk, add the wine and salt and pepper. Drop in the scallops and stir rapidly for 2-3 minutes.

Turn out onto hot shells and dust with paprika and chopped parsley.

CHARLIE'S QUEENIES IN CHEESE SAUCE

1lb/450g Queenies
½ pint/425ml Milk
1oz/25g Butter
1oz/25g Plain flour
2oz/50g Manx Cheddar Cheese, grated
A good Pinch of Curry Powder
Salt and Pepper
2oz/50g Prawns, shelled

Heat the oven to Gas Mark 4/180° C/350° F. Put the queenies into a shallow pan and cover with the milk. Simmer over a low heat for 5 minutes. Drain the queenies, reserving the milk. Put aside. Melt the butter in the pan and work in the flour. Cook over a low heat for 1 minute and gradually add the warm milk. Stir over a low heat until the sauce thickens. Remove from the heat and add the Manx Cheddar Cheese, and season with the curry powder, salt and pepper. Stir in the queenies and prawns.

Serve on a bed of rice or with pasta.

MANX DRESSED CRAB

2lb/1kg Crabs
Salt and Pepper
1 tsp Dry Mustard
2 hard boiled Eggs, separated
Lettuce leaves to garnish

Put the crabs in a large saucepan and just cover with salted water. Bring slowly to the boil, then simmer for 30 minutes. Drain and cool. Remove the large claws, them twist off the small ones and remove the undershells. Take out the small sacks from the crab's shells, any green matter and the spongy lungs from around the large shell. Scrape the brown creamy part into a bowl. Remove the white meat and reserve the shells. Crack the large claws, remove the meat and shred it. Mix the brown creamy part with salt and pepper to taste and add the mustard. Place the brown mixture across the centre of the shells, with the white meat on either side. Chop the egg whites and yolks separately and garnish.
    Serve on a bed of lettuce.

    Do be careful handling the crabs before cooking - my mother in law still has the scars where a crab nipped her!

MANX TRAWLER PIE

1½ lb/675g Manx White Fish
8oz/225g Kipper, filleted
1 Onion, coarsely chopped
1 pint/600ml Milk
1oz/25g Butter
1oz/25g Flour
2 tbsp/30g fresh chopped Parsley
12oz/350g Puff Pastry
1 Egg, beaten to glaze

Poach the fish and onion in milk for 10 minutes. Drain, reserve the milk. Remove the skin and bone from the fish, and set fish aside. Melt the butter in a pan, remove from the heat and stir in the flour. Cook, stirring for 1 minute; gradually stir in the milk. Cook, stirring until sauce thickens. Fold in the fish and parsley and season to taste. Spoon into a 2 pint/ 1.5 litre pie dish. Roll out the pastry and cut a strip to fit the rim. Dampen the rim and top with the remaining pastry. Seal the edges.

Glaze with a beaten egg and bake at Gas Mark 7/220° C/425° F for 30-35 minutes, until puffed and golden.

Alternatively, top with 2lb mashed potatoes.

MANX CHEESE

The Island's pedigree cattle create milk and cream of the highest quality. Milks used to produce superb quality cheese, using no artificial additives; without doubt it is amongst the finest in the world!

Manx Mild Cheddar was awarded 1st prize in the premier cheese show in the United Kingdom, also Reserve Champion of the show for all classes.

Traditional cheeses available:

Manx Cheshire
Manx Mild Cheddar
Manx Mature Cheddar
Manx Red Leicester
Manx Double Gloucester
Manx Smoked Cheddar (available in 6oz wheel wrapped in black wax)

NELLIE'S CHEESE PIE

4oz/115g Manx Cheddar Cheese
1lb/450g Potatoes, peeled and cut into cube sized pieces
8oz/225g Onions, peeled
2oz/50g Butter or Margarine
Salt
Freshly ground Pepper

Grate the cheese and set aside. Slice the potatoes and the onions and set these aside. Melt the butter or margarine in a large, heavy frying pan (skillet). Make layers of the potatoes, onions and cheese in the skillet, ending with a potato layer. Season each layer well with salt and pepper. Cover the skillet with a lid or foil. Cook over a low heat for about 40 minutes or until all the vegetables are cooked. Sprinkle the top with the remaining cheese and brown quickly under the grill.

Serve cut in wedges.

HOP-TU-NAA PASTIES

Today, Manx children celebrate Hop-Tu-Naa on the 31st October, travelling in small groups from house to house, singing traditional songs carrying turnip lanterns. Traditionally, the meal on Hollantide Eve was mashed fish, turnips and potatoes; the lantern providing the turnip!

My Hop-Tu-Naa pasties use cheese, not fish.

8oz/225g Turnip
1 small Onion
2 medium Potatoes
4oz/100g Manx Mild Cheddar Cheese

1 pinch Sage
½ tsp Salt
¼ tsp Pepper
1lb/450g Pastry, Wholemeal or White

Chop the potato and onion into small pieces and add to the turnip. Cook, using very little water in a pan with a close fitting lid. When the vegetables are tender, strain off the water, then stir in the cheese, sage and seasoning to the mixture. Cut the pastry into rounds, brush the edges with water, spoon the filling into the centre, then draw up the edges to form a pasty. Place on a baking sheet and bake in an oven Gas Mark 6/210° C/400° F for about 15 minutes.

Ideal for the singers to nibble between houses!

CHEAT'S CHEESE SOUFFLE

8oz/225g Manx Red Leicester Cheese, grated
1 thick slice of White Bread, cubed
7fl oz/200ml Milk
8 slices White Bread, crusts removed
3 tblsp Manx Butter
3 Eggs, separated
1½ tblsp Flour
½ tsp Salt
¼ tsp grated Nutmeg
3 rashers of Bacon, crisped and crumbled
4fl oz/100ml Single Cream

Preheat the oven to Gas Mark 4/180°C/350°F. Put the bread cubes in a shallow dish and sprinkle over half the milk. In another dish, spread out the bread slices and sprinkle them with the remaining milk. Leave the cubes and slices to soak. In a large bowl, cream the butter with a wooden spoon and mix in the egg yolks, one at a time. Stir in the flour. Add the soaked breadcrumbs and the cheese, salt and nutmeg. Blend well and stir in the cream. In a medium sized bowl, beat the egg whites with a wire whisk until they are stiff. Fold them into the cheese mixture. Line a greased straight sided, ovenproof dish or casserole with the soaked bread slices. Pour the cheese mixture into the dish. Bake in the oven for 35-40 minutes.

Top with the crispy bacon and serve immediately.

POTTED BEEF

8oz/225g lean Manx Beef
4oz/115g Streaky Bacon
½ tsp Salt
1 pint/600 ml Stock
Pinch Cayenne Pepper

Pinch Nutmeg
1 tsp Mustard
2oz/50g Butter
1 Bay Leaf or Rosemary

Cut the beef and bacon into small pieces. Add the salt and stock and simmer for 30-40 minutes until tender. When cooked put through blender/mincer. Add all the remaining ingredients except the butter and herbs. Melt the butter and add half to the meat mixture. Mix well and pack into small pots. Place bay leave or rosemary on top and pour over the rest of the butter. Keep in the refrigerator and eat within 2-3 days. Serve with a salad or just on hot brown toast.

BREWERY STEW

2lb/1kg Stewing Beef, cut into 2"/5cm cubes
2 tblsp Seasoned Flour
2oz/50g Butter
½ pint/275ml Water
4oz/100g Mushrooms
1lb/450g Carrots, sliced lengthwise

1½ lb/675g Onions, chopped
¾ pint/450ml Okells Nut Brown Ale
Salt and Pepper
Pinch of Marjoram
1-2 tblsp Brown Sugar

Toss the meat in the seasoned flour to coat lightly. Melt half the butter in a frying pan and fry the cubes of meat until brown. Transfer to a saucepan or flameproof casserole. Pour half the water into the frying pan to remove the sediment and add to the meat. Melt the remaining butter in the frying pan and fry the onions, mushrooms and carrots over a medium heat until brown. Add the vegetables to the meat and deglaze the pan as before with the remaining water. Season with salt and pepper, add the marjoram and Nut Brown Ale. Put the saucepan or casserole on the heat, bring to the boil, cover and simmer very gently for a further 30 minutes. Serve with baked potatoes or new potatoes in their jackets.

SULBY POT ROAST

2lb/1kg Joint (Flank, Top Rib or Chunk) Manx Beef
4 tblsp/60ml Oil
2 carrots, sliced
2 small Parsnips, sliced
1 stick Celery, chopped
3fl oz/75ml Glen Kella Whiskey

Heat the oven to Gas Mark 4/180°C/350°F. If possible use a casserole in which the meat can be fried and roasted, or use a frying pan and transfer the meat and fat to an earthenware casserole to pot roast. Brown the joint well in oil. Add the vegetables around the joint and pour in the whiskey. Cover with a well fitting lid. Cook for about 2 hours, turning the joint once, until the meat is tender. Remove the meat to a heated serving dish. Use the cooking liquor, diluted with water and suitably thickened for a sauce or gravy.

SHEPHERD'S PIE

1½ lb/675g Potatoes
2 tblsp Dripping
1 Onion, chopped
4oz/115g Mushrooms, sliced
1¼ lb/565g Cooked Manx Lamb, minced

2 large Tomatoes, chopped (or half a can)
½ tsp Dry Mustard
Salt and Pepper
5fl oz/150ml well seasoned Gravy
1oz/25g Butter

Cook the potatoes in boiling, salted water for 15 to 20 minutes, or until they are tender. Meanwhile heat the dripping in a saucepan. Add the onion and mushrooms and fry for 5 minutes. Stir in the lamb, tomatoes, mustard, salt and pepper to taste. Pour over the gravy and bring to the boil. Simmer for 5 minutes, them transfer to a pie dish. Drain the potatoes, then mash with the butter and salt and pepper to taste. Spoon over the mixture in the dish, then put into the oven preheated to Gas Mark 4/180° C/350° F. Bake for 20-25 minutes, or until the potatoes are browned.

Traditionally Monday's meal, using Sunday's roast lamb. However, minced beef can be substituted.

VAL'S PRESSED SILVERSIDE

My father's favourite

4lb/2kg Silverside Manx Beef
1 bottle Okells Pale Ale
2 Onions
1 Bay Leaf
6 Peppercorns
4 Cloves, stuck into the onions

Soak the beef in water for 2 hours then drain. Place the beef in a large ovenproof casserole, add all the remaining ingredients, pour in the Pale Ale and, if needed, a little water to cover the beef. Cover and put in a preheated oven Gas Mark 4/170° C/350° F. Cook for 3-4 hours until the meat is tender. Remove the beef from the casserole, place between two plates with a heavy weight on the top plate, leave to stand overnight.

Serve cold, thinly sliced with fresh green salad.

A lovely sandwich or Picnic meat.

SWEET MANX LAMB

All plain cuts of meat can be glazed with Manx honey while roasting. It also gives the meat an attractive appearance.

1 tblsp Manx Honey
1 tsp Orange Juice
1 tsp Lemon Juice

To serve
Chopped Rosemary

Roast the lamb according to your taste, but 15 minutes before the end of cooking time drain off the fat from the roasting dish and pour the combined honey, orange and lemon juice over the meat. Return the meat to the oven and baste frequently until the end of the cooking time. Add the chopped rosemary to the pan juices and serve separately as a sauce.

I use this glaze for baked Manx Gammon, but replace the rosemary with fresh parsley.

LAMB STEW WITH PARSLEY DUMPLINGS

2lb/1kg Best end of neck Manx Lamb Chops (trimmed of excess fat)
2oz/50g Seasoned Flour
1oz/25g Dripping
2 Onions, chopped
2 Carrots, sliced
1 large Cooking Apple, cored and chopped
1 pint/600ml Water
1 Chicken or Vegetable Stock Cube

Dumplings
4oz/125g Sunrise Self Raising Flour
½ tsp Salt
2 tsp Butter
3fl oz/75ml Milk
1 tblsp finely chopped Parsley

Coat the lamb chops with seasoned flour, heat the dripping in a large stew pan. Add the chops and brown well, add the onions and carrots and fry for a few minutes dissolve the stock cube in the water and add to the chops and vegetables. Add the apple, season to taste, cover and simmer for 1 hour. Make the dumplings, sift the flour and salt together. Rub in the butter, then stir in the parsley, add sufficient milk to make a soft dough. Drop a tablespoonful of the dumpling mixture into the simmering stew and cook for a further 20 minutes.

I make this meal in minutes in my pressure cooker, when I was first married a best end of neck cost one shilling, yesterday I paid £1.65 for a lovely best end, so its still an inexpensive meal today.

PORK FILLET PHIONA

This recipe uses expensive pork fillet, but the tasty filling makes the meat go twice as far. A super dinner party meat course!

1 large tenderloin of Manx Pork
1lb/450g Puff Pastry (I use frozen)

Stuffing
1lb/450g diced Manx Pork or Pork Scraps
1 medium Onion
1 large Cooking Apple
8oz/225g White Bread
2 tsp/50g Sage
Salt and Pepper
1 glass White Wine

I used to use a mincer for this recipe, now I have a food processor, but before now I have chopped the stuffing with a sharp knife. Chop, blend or mince all the stuffing ingredients, moisten with wine to combine.

Roll out the pastry to a rectangle large enough to cover the fillet; place the pastry on a baking tray and lay the pork fillet on the pastry. Split the fillet down the centre with a sharp knife cutting down about three quarters through. Place your thumbs down the centre split, then squeeze each side to flatten slightly. Push the stuffing into the slit and fold the fillet over.

Moisten the pastry edges, seal the pastry, decorate with pastry leaves, brush with beaten egg and bake at Gas Mark 6/210° C/400° F for 30 minutes.

Serve with new potatoes and fresh vegetables.

One of the delightful walks that interlace the Island, a morning stroll or a serious hike, the Isle of Man is a wonderland for walkers. Footpaths cross the wild hills and moorland or follow the spectacular coastal way, a rich variety of bird life and a wealth of archaeological remains, many left by the Vikings who raided the Island over one thousand years ago and found it so pleasant that they stayed for thre hundred years, integrating their culture with the local Celts.

From simple village to grand castle, the Isle of Man provides a fascinating glimpse of the past.

MANX RABBIT IN ONION SAUCE

An inexpensive meal, but so much tastier than frozen chicken. If you have never tried rabbit this is a dish to try, my brothers favourite meal.

1 Rabbit (ask the butcher to joint it)
4oz/115g Bacon
1 tblsp Vinegar
1 Onion, peeled and quartered
1 Carrot, sliced
1 Bay Leaf
A Sprig of Thyme (½ tsp, dried)
1 pint/600ml half Milk, half Water

<u>For the sauce</u>
1 finely chopped Onion
1oz/25g Flour
1oz/25g Butter
Black Pepper and Salt to taste

Wipe the rabbit with the vinegar and rinse in water, place in a heavy saucepan with chopped bacon, onion, carrot, bay leaf and thyme, cover with milk and water. Simmer until tender, about 1½ hours on top of stove much less in the pressure cooker. Lift out the rabbit, remove all bones, lift out the bacon, place together on a serving dish. Use the strained stock to make the sauce. Simmer the finely chopped onion in a little stock until tender and drain.

Melt the butter in a clean pan, gradually add the flour and strained rabbit stock to make about half pint/300ml. To make the sauce add the cooked onion, salt and pepper to taste. Pour sauce over the rabbit, keep hot in the oven and serve with fresh vegetables and a triangle of puffed pastry cooked separately, or with a portion of saffron rice.

Red currant jelly is a tasty accompaniment.

TRADITIONAL MANX RABBIT PIE

1½ lb/675g boned Rabbit pieces
2oz/50g Seasoned Flour
2oz/50g Dripping
10fl oz/300ml Chicken Stock
4oz/115g finely chopped Bacon
2 Carrots, chopped

2 Onions, chopped
1 tsp Thyme
Salt and Pepper
8oz/225g Shortcrust Pastry
1 tblsp Milk

Roll the rabbit pieces in the seasoned flour. Heat the dripping in a saucepan. Add the rabbit pieces and brown on all sides. Add the stock, bacon, carrots, onions, thyme and salt and pepper, and stir to mix. Bring to the boil. Simmer until the rabbit is cooked through. Transfer to a large pie dish and leave until cold. Roll out the pastry dough until it is as large as the pie dish. Cover the pie dish with the dough, trimming off the ends to fit. Brush the pastry with the milk. Put into a preheated oven Gas Mark 5/190°C/375°F and bake for 30-35 minutes, or until the pastry is a deep golden brown.

Called Calf pie in our house, I did not know I was eating rabbit for years, presumably the name came about because of the amount of rabbits on the Calf of Man.

ROAST GOOSE

Traditionally, roast goose was eaten on Michaelmas Day (29th September), however, I have only known it at Christmas. Just writing this recipe reminds me of the clouds of feathers as we plucked the Christmas goose; and the endless jars filled with goose grease, creamy yellow fat. I have never suffered from a chest cold and am sure it is because of those jars full of glistening fat; the thought of having that rubbed all over my chest kept the wheezing well away! However, grease apart, goose is rather neglected in favour of turkey today - but there is no comparison in the flavour!

1 large Goose
1 Lemon
1 Onion
Sprigs of Sage

Scald the goose with boiling water inside and out, prick the skin with a fork and rub all over with half of the lemon. Dust the goose with salt and pepper and place the halves of lemon, onion and sage in the cavity. Place goose on a trivet in the roasting dish and cook in a very hot oven for 20 minutes; reduce heat and cook for 2-3 hours at Gas Mark 4/160° C/350° F. Remove excess fat during cooking.

Serve the goose with apple sauce, mustard, boiled potatoes and peas or broad beans.

BONNAG

Traditionally cooked on a griddle over an open fire

1lb/450g Flour
¼ tsp Soda
¼ tsp Cream of Tartar
Salt
Buttermilk

Mix all the dry ingredients together and rub in lard until there are fine crumbs. Soften this with buttermilk. Form this into 3 round loaves and cook these in a moderately hot oven for about 1 hour.

A fruit bonnag is made with the addition of 3oz/200g of currants.

BROWN SODA BREAD
or
WHEATEN BREAD

Traditional Manx country bread, made without yeast. The buttermilk is very important, as well as activating the raising agents it keeps the bread moist and gives it flavour.

1lb/450g Pioneer Wholemeal Flour
1 tsp Bicarbonate of Soda
1 tsp Cream of Tartar
1½ tsp Salt
1oz/25g Butter
½ pint/300ml Buttermilk

Preheat the oven to Gas Mark 8/225° C/425° F. Mix the flour, bicarbonate of soda, cream of tartar and salt together. Rub in the butter. Pour the buttermilk into the flour. Now work quickly and knead well on a floured board for a few minutes. Shape into a flattened round and cut a cross right across the middle with a floured knife. Sprinkle the top lightly with flour and place carefully on a greased baking sheet. Bake for 30-40 minutes, until golden and cooked through. When cooked the loaf will sound hollow when tapped. Remove to a rack, cover the loaf lightly with a slightly damp cloth and allow to cool.

Eat sliced with butter, preferably the same day as it is made.

I've never understood people rushing out to buy bread when a Bank Holiday occurs, it is a perfect excuse for making what I call easy bread.

In the old days a goose wing was used to draw the cross and form the farls (quarters).

FARMHOUSE FRUIT CAKE

8oz/225g Sunrise Self Raising Flour
4oz/115g Sugar
12oz/300g Mixed Fruit
2 beaten Eggs
4oz/115g Manx Butter
½ tsp Nutmeg
1 tsp Mixed Spice
¼ tsp Ground Cinnamon
4fl oz/120ml Milk

Preheat the oven to Gas Mark 3/160° C/325° F. Place all the ingredients, except the fruit, into a bowl and beat by hand for 5 minutes, add the mixed fruit. Turn into a greased and floured 6 or 7 inch cake tin and bake for 2 hours. Cool in the tin.

A speedily made cake that cooks, whilst Mrs Clucas, Mrs Cooil or Mrs Maddrell get on with the numerous jobs of a farmer's wife.

MANX CARROT CAKE

Carrots were originally used as a sweetener in cake making, but this is a modern recipe

8oz/225g Sunrise Self Raising Flour
Pinch of Salt
2 tsp Ground Cinnamon
6oz/165g Castor Sugar
8fl oz/225ml Sunflower Oil
4 Eggs
6oz/165g Manx Carrots, grated

<u>For the topping</u>
1oz/25g Butter
5oz/140g Cream Cheese
8oz/225g Icing Sugar
2 drops Vanilla Essence

Preheat the oven to Gas Mark 4/180° C/350° F. Grease and line a 9 inch/23cm square cake tin. Sift the flour, salt and cinnamon and then beat in the oil, add the eggs one at a time. Add the carrots and stir in. Pour the batter into the lined tin and bake in the preheated oven for about 1 hour or until the cake is firm to the touch and well risen. Turn out onto a wire rack and allow to cool. Meanwhile, make the topping. Beat the butter until soft, then blend in the cream cheese. Beat in the icing sugar and the vanilla essence. Spread over the top and the sides of the cake making a pattern with a palette knife. Cut into slices.

CHURCH FETE CHOCOLATE CAKE

6oz/175g Manx Butter, softened
9oz/250g Dark Soft Brown Sugar
2 level tblsp Golden Syrup
3 Eggs
2½ oz/60g Cocoa Powder
4fl oz/125ml warm Water
9oz/250g Pioneer Plain Flour
3 level tsp Baking Powder
4oz/125g Natural Yogurt

<u>For the chocolate icing</u>
6oz/175g Plain Cake Chocolate
3oz/75g Manx Butter
3fl oz/75ml Double Cream

<u>For the filling</u>
2 tblsp Strawberry Jam
7fl oz/200ml Double Cream

Preheat the oven to Gas Mark 2/160° C/300° F. Grease and line a 9 inch/23cm round cake tin with greaseproof paper. Place the butter in a large bowl and beat until very soft. Gradually beat in the sugar until light and fluffy, then stir in the syrup. Lightly whisk the eggs and gradually add into the mixture, blending well after each addition. Blend the cocoa with the the water until smooth, then gradually blend into the mixture, making sure all the ingredients are incorporated. Sift the flour and baking powder together and fold in, with the yogurt, adding a little at a time to make a smooth mixture and put in the lined cake tin. Place in the oven and cook for approximately 1½ hours, or until a skewer pushed into the centre of the cake comes clean. Remove from the oven, and cool in the tin for half an hour. Turn out and cool on a wire rack. To make the chocolate icing, break the chocolate into pieces. Melt in a heatproof basin over a pan of hot water on a low heat. Cut the butter into small pieces and stir into the chocolate. Stir in the cream and mix.

To finish the cake, split horizontally into layers and spread each cut side with the strawberry jam. Whip the cream and use to sandwich the layers together. When the chocolate is firm enough to spread, to ice the top and sides of the cake, smoothing with a palette knife. Swirl into a design.

CREGNEISH CRUNCHIES

4oz/115g Manx Butter
1oz/25g Soft Brown Sugar
3 tblsp Clear Honey
8oz/225g Rolled Oats

Melt the margarine, sugar and honey in a pan over a medium heat. Stir in the oats until coated. Spoon into a lightly oiled 7.5 inch/19cm square tin. Bake at Gas Mark 5/190° C/ 375° F for 30-40 minutes until golden. Cool slightly and then cut into 12 bars. Cool completely in the tin, store in an airtight container.

Alternative
Substitute 8oz/225g Unsweetened Muesli for the rolled oats in the mixture. Spread into a lightly oiled, 7.5 inch x 11.5 inch (19cm x 29cm) Swiss Roll tin. Bake for 30 minutes. Cool slightly and cut into 16 bars. Store in an airtight container.

ELSIE'S BUNLOAF

1½ lb/675g Plain Flour
8oz/225g Raisins
8oz/225g Currants
8oz/225g Sultanas
8oz/225g Mixed Peel
8oz/225g Sugar

10oz/275g Butter or Margarine
½ tsp Mixed Spice
½ tsp Cinnamon
1 tblsp Syrup
2 tsp Bicarbonate of Soda
1 pint/600ml Buttermilk

Sieve all the dry ingredients and rub in fat. Add sugar, mixed peel and fruit. Put bicarbonate of soda in a basin and mix smoothly with the milk. Pour into the dry ingredients. Finally, add the syrup and mix thoroughly. Put into a greased baking tin and bake in a moderate oven for 2 hours.

I've never made this bunloaf, but every year I get this lovely bunloaf as a present; this year I asked for the recipe.

MANX CHRISTMAS PUDDING

4oz/115g Currants
8oz/225g Raisins
8oz/225g Sultanas
4oz/115g Chopped Mixed Peel
1 small Cooking Apple, finely chopped
1 Manx Carrot, finely grated
3fl oz/75ml Castletown Nut Brown Ale
Juice and rind of 1 Lemon
6oz/175g Butter
8oz/225g Soft Brown Sugar
2 Eggs
8oz/225g fresh Brown Breadcrumbs
2 tsp Ground Mixed Spice
1 tsp Grated Nutmeg
½ tsp Ground Ginger

Mix the fruit, ale, lemon juice, rind, apple and carrot and together. Cover and leave overnight.

Cream the butter and sugar together until fluffy. Beat in the eggs, then add all the remaining ingredients and mix well. Put in the centre of a floured pudding cloth and tie securely, allowing room for expansion. Put into a large pan, half filled with hot water and boil the pudding for 4 hours. When cool, wrap in a clean cloth to store.

I pressure cook my pudding in a well buttered basin.
Our pudding was always made on November 1st, unless it was a Sunday.

SUMMER
or
NEXT TO NOTHING PUDDING

Spend a lovely sunny afternoon collecting blackberries, wash thoroughly. Cook the blackberries with sugar to taste. Slice white bread and cut off crusts, line a 2pt/1.2 litre pudding basin with the slices of bread, pour in the fruit and the juice up to the brim. Cover with a layer of bread slices, place a saucer on top of the pudding and weigh it down. Refrigerate overnight.

To serve turn out onto a plate and serve with delicious Manx cream.

Strawberries, Raspberries, Redcurrants or Blackcurrants can be used instead of Blackberries.

WILDFLOWER PUDDING

Meadowsweet, as the name suggests, imparts a honeyed sweetness when stewed with fruits.

4 flowerheads of Meadowsweet (pick a few extra to garnish)
1lb/450g Fruit (plums, apricots or cherries)
1 glass White Wine

Halve and stone the fruit, then simmer for approximately 10 minutes with the flowers and the wine.
    Serve hot.

FENELLA'S ELDERFLOWER CHAMPAGNE

1 gallon cold Water
1½ lb/560g Sugar
7 heads of Elderflower
2 Lemons
2 tblsp/30ml White Wine Vinegar

Bring water to the boil and pour over the sugar. When cold, add the flowerheads, lemon slices and the white wine vinegar. Cover and leave to stand for 24 hours. Strain and bottle, using strong bottles.

Cork well as this wine is very fizzy, true to its name. Keep this 14 days before drinking.

ELDERBERRY WATER ICE

6oz/165g Sugar
1lb/450g Elderberries
Squeeze of Lemon Juice

To serve
Sparkling sweet Elderberry Wine (champagne)

In a heavy based saucepan, dissolve the sugar in ½ pint/300ml water. Bring to the boil and boil for 5 minutes. Stir in the elderberries and simmer until tender. Puree the elderberries and pass through a fine sieve into a bowl. strain in the lemon juice to taste. Chill for 30 minutes and pour into a container. Cover and freeze until firm, beating 3 times at 45 minute intervals. About 30 minutes before serving, transfer the water ice to refrigerator. Pour some sparkling elderberry wine over each portion as it is served.

Serving suggestion: Scoop into tall, slim, frosted wine glasses and trickle over a little elderflower 'champagne' or wine.

FRESH STRAWBERRIES IN ELDERFLOWER SYRUP

2lb/1kg Strawberries, freshly picked and hulled
1 pint/600ml Water
5oz/140g Granulated Sugar
Pared Rind and Juice of 2 Lemons
3 handfuls of Elderflower

Gently dissolve the sugar in the water and lemon rind. Boil this fast for 5 minutes, draw the pan off the heat, add the juice of 2 lemons and 3 handfuls of elderflower (no need to pluck the flowers from the stalks as the syrup is strained). Leave to cool and then strain through a sieve.

Pour this onto the strawberries which have been arranged in a serving dish. Leave the strawberries to absorb the flavour for at least 2 hours.

Elderflowers impart a delicate flavour to strawberry jam.

BRAMBLE JELLY

Put the brambles in a pan and just cover them with water. If you haven't got too many brambles, you can pad out the quantities by adding some cored and roughly chopped apples which also help the setting. Simmer the fruit and water together until the fruit is really soft and disintigrating into the water. Remove from the heat and have a large bowl ready, into which you strain the contents of the pan through a jelly bag or piece of muslin or cheesecloth. When as much juice as possible has been dripped and squeezed from the cloth, measure the liquid and pour it into a rinsed out saucepan. For each 1 pint/600ml add 1lb/450g granulated or preserving sugar. Over a low heat, dissolve the sugar completely in the fruit juice, then bring to the boil and boil fast.

After 10 minutes' boiling, drop some onto a cold saucer, pull the pan off the heat while you wait for the jelly on the saucer to set. If you push the surface with your fingertip and the surface wrinkles, you have a set. If it does not wrinkle, replace the pan on the heat and boil fast for a further few minutes and test again.

Using a small jug or ladle with a lip, pour the jelly into warmed jars, cover with waxed paper discs and seal with cellophane and rubber bands when cold.

GLEN KELLA MARMALADE

1½ lb/675g Lemons
2½ pints/1.5l Water
3lb/1.5kg Sugar
1 miniature bottle Glen Kella whiskey

Scrub the lemons, cut in half and squeeze out the juice. Place the pips in a muslin bag. Slice the fruit finely and place in a preserving pan with the juice, muslin bag and water. Simmer gently until tender (about 2 hours). Squeeze the muslin bag to extract the juice, then remove the bag. Remove from the heat. Add the sugar and stir until dissolved. Return to the heat. Bring to the boil rapidly until setting point is reached. Stir in the whiskey. Remove any scum. Allow to cool slightly until a skin is formed. Stir gently and pour into warmed jars, cover and label.

The crystal clear Glen Kella Whiskey adds a taste sensation to this pale lemon marmalade.

AUNTY MURIEL'S MANX HONEY FUDGE

12oz/340g Sugar
4oz/115g Manx Honey
14oz can Full Cream Condensed (Sweetened) Milk
2oz/50g Butter or Margarine
¼ pint/150ml Water
1 tsp Vanilla Essence

Put all the ingredients into a strong saucepan. Stir over a low heat until the sugar has dissolved. Boil steadily, stirring only occasionally (to prevent the mixture burning), until the fudge reaches 'soft ball' stage or 114° C/238° F. Remove the pan from the heat and beat until the mixture just begins to thicken and becomes opaque (cloudy) in appearance. This is very important when making fudge. Grease a 8 inch square sandwich tin with a little melted butter. Pour in the fudge and leave until almost set; cut into neat pieces with a sharp knife. Leave in the tin until quite firm.

A dear friend makes 'melt in the mouth' fudge, I have fond memories of her father in his dark suit and winged collar - every inch the 'official' taster.

CINDER TOFFEE

1lb/500g Golden Syrup
8oz/250g Brown Sugar
2oz/50g Butter
2 tblsp Vinegar
1 tsp Baking Soda

Use a large, heavy non stick saucepan, slowly melt all the ingredients except the baking soda, boil without stirring until a drop hardens in a cup of cold water. At 190° C on a sugar thermometer, switch off. Carefully stir in the baking soda, which will cause the toffee to foam up. Pour toffee onto a greased board, fold outer edges towards the middle, pull and repeat until the toffee turns pale yellow. Put into a greased tin, mark into small bars and allow to harden.

The marble slab was the ideal place to 'pull the toffee', I still have a scar over my eye where I caught the corner of the slab whilst trying to avoid being reprimanded for stealing toffee off the 'slab'!

INDEX

A	Annies soused Herring		5
B	Beef	Bonnag	33
		Brewery Stew	22
		Potted Beef	21
		Pressed Silverside	25
		Shepherds Pie	24
		Sulby Pot Roast	25
	Bramble Jelly		46
	Bunloaf		49
C	Cakes	Farmhouse Fruit	35
		Carrot Cake	36
		Church Fete Chocolate Cake	37
	Cheats cheese Souffle		19
	Cheese Pie		17
	Cheese & onion Soup		3
	Christmas Pudding		40
	Cinder Toffee		48
	Crab		14
	Cregneish Crunchies		38
E	Elderflower Champagne		44
	Elderflower with Strawberries		45
	Elderflower Water Ice		44
F	Farmhouse Fruit Cake		35
	Fudge (Aunty Muriels)		48
G	Goose (Roast)		32
	Glen Kella Marmalade		47
H	Hop-tu-naa Pasties		18
K	Kipper Kedegree		6
	Kipper Mousse		10

		Kipper Pate	8
		Kipper Salad	8
L	Lamb	Lamb Stew with Parsley Dumplings	27
		Sweet Manx Lamb	26
M	Manx Broth		1
	Manx Rabbit Pie		31
	Manx Crab		14
	Marmalade (Glen Kella)		47
P	Peel Hot Pot		11
	Pork Fillet Phionna		28
	Potted Beef		21
	P.O.W. Soup		2
Q	Queenies	Queenies in Cheese Sauce	13
		Queenies Port le Moirrey	13
R	Rabbit	Rabbit in Onion Sauce	30
		Traditional Manx Rabbit Pie	31
S	Shepherds Pie		24
	Soups	Cheese & Onion	3
		Manx Broth	1
		P.O.W. Soup	2
	Spud 'n' Herrin'		4
	Sulby Pot Roast		23
	Summer Pudding		42
	Sweet Manx Lamb		26
T	Toffee Cinder		48
	Traditional Manx Rabbit Pie		31
	Trawler Pie		15
V	Vals Pressed Silverside		25
W	Wheaten Bread		34
	Wildflower Pudding		43